JIMMY ROLLINS

Joe Gaspar

PowerKiDS press

New York

Published in 2011 by The Rosen Publishing Group, Inc.
29 East 21st Street, New York, NY 10010

First Edition

Editor: Amelie von Zumbusch
Book Design: Kate Laczynski
Photo Researcher: Jessica Gerweck

Photo Credits: Cover, p. 1 Jim McIsaac/Getty Images; p. 4 Drew Hallowell/Getty Images; p. 7 Stephen Dunn/Getty Images; p. 8 Al Bello/Getty Images Sport/Getty Images; p. 11 Ezra Shaw/Getty Images; p. 12 Harry How/Getty Images; p.15 Mitchell Layton/ Getty Images; p. 16 Brad Mangin/MLB via Getty Images; p. 19 Rich Pilling/MLB via Getty Images; p. 20 Elsa/Getty Images; p. 22 Nick Laham/Getty Images.

Library of Congress Cataloging-in-Publication Data

Gaspar, Joe.
  Jimmy Rollins / Joe Gaspar. — 1st ed.
     p. cm. — (Baseball's mvps)
  Includes index.
  ISBN 978-1-4488-0631-7 (library binding) —
ISBN 978-1-4488-1786-3 (pbk.) — ISBN 978-1-4488-1787-0
(6-pack)
  1. Rollins, Jimmy—Juvenile literature. 2. Baseball players—United States—Biography—Juvenile literature. I. Title.
GV865.R64G37 2011
  796.357092—dc22
  [B]
                    2009050867

Manufactured in the United States of America

CPSIA Compliance Information: Batch #WS10PK: For Further Information contact Rosen Publishing, New York, New York at 1-800-237-9932

CONTENTS

4

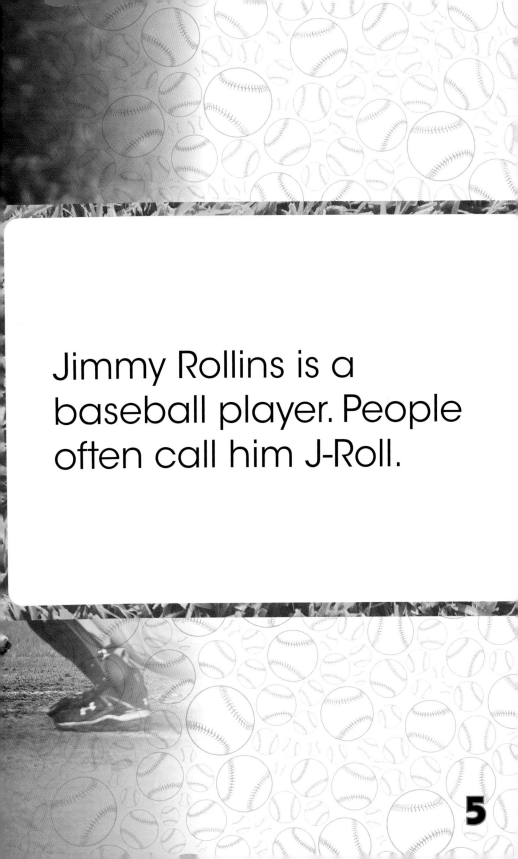

Jimmy Rollins is a baseball player. People often call him J-Roll.

Rollins was born in Oakland, California. He was born on November 27, 1978.

Oakland

8

Rollins plays for the Philadelphia Phillies. He is the team's shortstop.

Rollins played his first game with the Phillies in 2000.

11

The Phillies have many good players. Rollins likes his teammates.

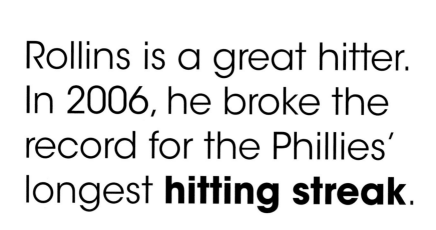

Rollins is a great hitter. In 2006, he broke the record for the Phillies' longest **hitting streak**.

15

16

Rollins is very fast! This makes him good at stealing bases.

In 2007, Rollins was named the National **League** MVP, or most **valuable** player.

19

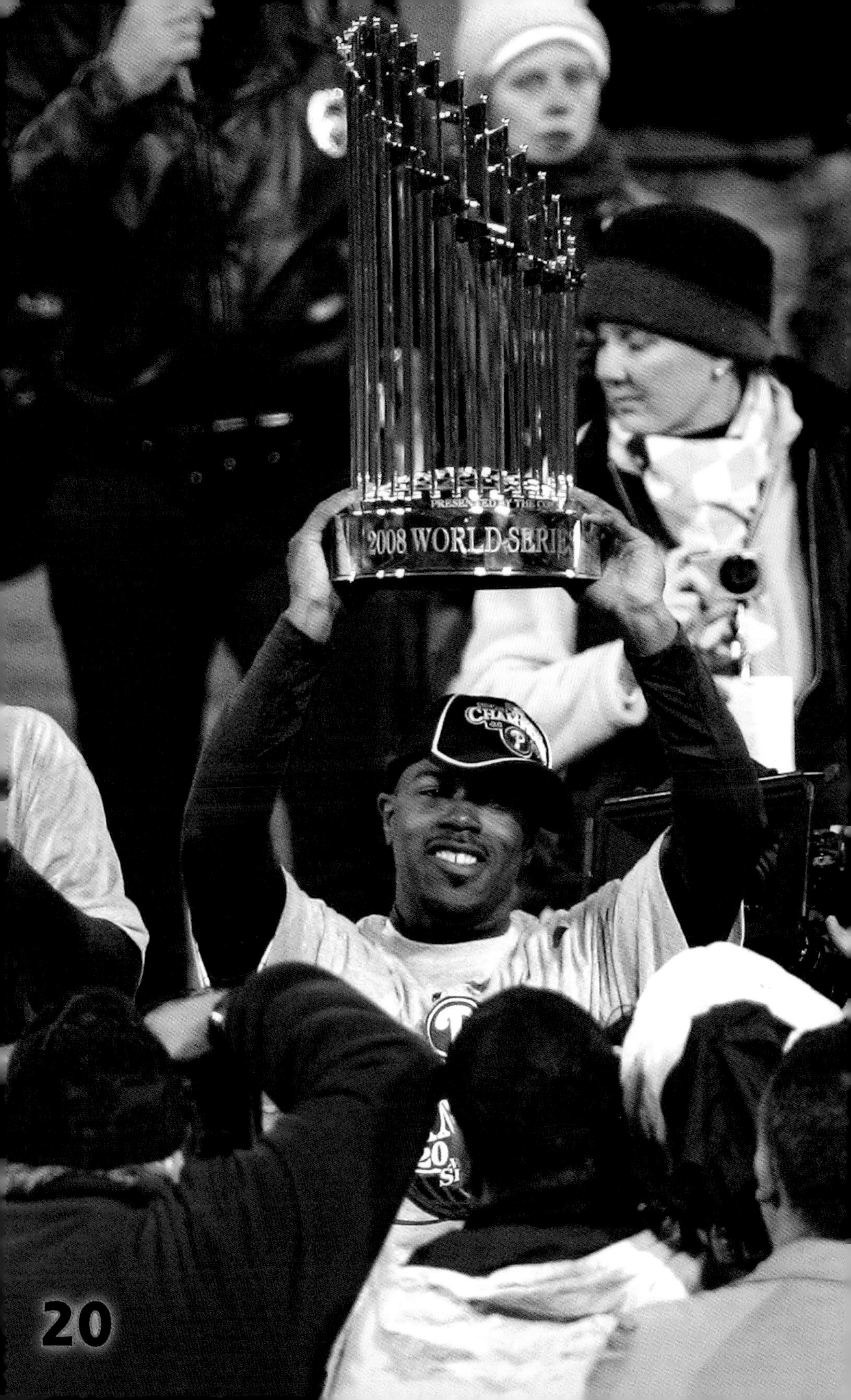
2008 WORLD SERIES

In 2008, he helped the Phillies win the **World Series**.

Today, Rollins is one of baseball's biggest stars!

BOOKS

Here are more books to read about Jimmy Rollins and baseball:

Frisch, Aaron. *Philadelphia Phillies.* World Series Champions. Mankato, MN: Creative Education, Inc., 2008.

Kelley, K. C. *Philadelphia Phillies.* Favorite Baseball Teams. Mankato, MN: The Child's World, Inc., 2010.

WEB SITES

Due to the changing nature of Internet links, PowerKids Press has developed an online list of Web sites related to the subject of this book. This site is updated regularly. Please use this link to access the list:
www.powerkidslinks.com/bmvp/jr/

GLOSSARY

hitting streak (HIT-ing STREEK) When a baseball player gets a hit in many games in a row.

league (LEEG) A group of sports teams.

valuable (VAL-yoo-bul) Important.

World Series (WURLD SEER-eez) A group of games in which the two best baseball teams play against each other.

INDEX